Lithobolia, or, The stone-throwing devil : being
an exact and true account (by way of journal) of
the various actions of infernal spirits, or (devils
incarnate) witches, or both, and the great disturbance
and amazement they gave to George Waltons...

R. C. (Richard Chamberlayne)

LITHOBOLIA:

OR, THE

Stone - Throwing Devil.

BEING

An Exact and True Account (by way of Journal) of the various Actions of Infernal Spirits, or (*Devils Incarnate*) Witches, or both; and the great Disturbance and Amazement they gave to *George Waltons* Family, at a place call'd *Great Island* in the Province of *New-Hantshire* in *New-England*, chiefly in Throwing about (by an Invisible hand) *Stones, Bricks*, and *Brick-bats* of all Sizes, with several other things, as *Hammers, Mauls, Iron-Crows, Spits*, and other Domestick Utensils, as came into their Hellish Minds, and this for the space of a Quarter of a Year.

By R. C. Esq; who was a Sojourner in the same Family the whole Time, and an Ocular Witness of these Diabolick Inventions.

The Contents hereof being manifestly known to the Inhabitants of that Province, and Persons of other Provinces, and is upon Record in his Majesties Council-Court held for that Province.

LONDON,
Printed, and are to be Sold by *E. Whitlook* near *Stationers-Hall,* 1698.

TO

The much Honoured

Mart. Lumley, Efq;

SIR,

AS the fubfequent Script deferves not to be
called a *Book*, fo thefe precedent Lines pre-
fume not to a *Dedication*: But, *Sir*, it is an occafion that I am ambitious to lay hold on, to difco-
ver to You by this Epitome (as it were) the pro-
penfion and inclination I have to give a more full
and perfect demonftration of the Honour, Love,
and Service, I own (as I think my felf oblig'd) to have
for You. To a Sober, Judicious, and well Princi-
pled Perfon, fuch as your Self, plain Truths are
much more agreeable than the moft charming and
furprifing *Romance* or *Novel*, with all the ftrange
turns and events. That this is of the firft fort, (as I
have formerly upon Record attefted) I do now aver
and proteft; yet neither is it lefs ftrange than true,

A 2   and

The Epiſtle Dedicatory.

and ſo may be capable of giving you ſome Diverſion for an hour: For this interruption of your more ſerious ones, I cannot doubt your candor and clemency, in pardoning it, that ſo well know (and do moſt ſenſibly acknowledg) your high Worth and Goodneſs; and that the Relation I am Dignified with, infers a mutual *Patronization*.

SIR, I am

Your moſt Humble Servant,

R. C.

To the much Honoured
R. F. Efq;

TO tell *ftrange feats of* Dæmons, *here I am;*
    Strange, but moft true they are, ev'n to a Dram,
Tho' Sadduceans *cry, 'tis all a Sham.*

Here's Stony Arg'uments of perfuafive Dint,
They'l not believe it, told, nor yet in Print:
What fhould the Reafon be? The Devil's in't.

And yet they wifh to be convinc'd by Sight,
Affur'd by Apparition of a Sprite;
But Learned Brown *doth ftate the matter right:*

Satan *will never Inftrumental be*
Of fo much Good, to Appear to them; for he
Hath them fure by their Infidelity.

But you, my Noble Friend, know better things;
Your Faith, mounted on Religions Wings,
Sets you above the Clouds whence Error fprings.

Your Soul reflecting on this lower Sphear,
Of froth and vanity, joys oft to-hear
The Sacred Ora'cles, where all Truths appear,

Which will Conduct out of this Labyrinth of Night,
And lead you to the fource of Intellect'ual Light.

Which is the Hearty Prayer of

Your moft faithful Humble Servant,

R.

LITHOBOLIA:

OR, THE

Stone-throwing Devil, &c.

SUCH is the Sceptical Humour of this Age for Incredulity, (not to say Infidelity,) That I wonder they do not take up and profess, in terms, the *Pyrrhonian* Doctrine of disbelieving their very Senses. For that which I am going to relate happening to cease in the Province of *New-Hampshire* in *America,* just upon that Governour's Arrival and Appearance at the Council there, who was informed by my self, and several other Gentlemen of the Council, and other considerable Persons, of the true and certain Reality hereof, yet he continued tenacious in the Opinion that we were all imposed upon by the waggery of some unlucky Boys; which, considering the Circumstances and Passages hereafter mentioned, was altogether impossible.

I have a Wonder to relate; for such (I take it) is so to be termed whatsoever is Præternatural, and not assignable to, or the effect of, Natural Causes: It is a *Lithobolia,* or *Stone-throwing,* which happened by *Witchcraft,* (as was supposed) and maliciously perpetrated by an *Elderly Woman,* a Neighbour suspected, and (I think) formerly detected for such kind of Diabolical Tricks and Practises; and the wicked Instigation did arise upon the account of some small quantity of Land in her Field, which she pretended was unjustly taken into the Land of the Person where the Scene of this Matter lay, and was her Right; she having been often very clamorous about that Affair, and heard to say, with much Bitterness, that her Neighbour (*innuendo* the fore-mentioned Person, his Name *George Walton*) should never quietly injoy that piece of Ground. Which, as it has confirm'd my self and others in the Opinion that there are such

things

things as *Witches*, and the Effects of *Witchcraft*, or at least of the mischievous Actions of *Evil Spirits*; which some do as little give Credit to, as in the Case of *Witches*, utterly rejecting both their *Operations* and their *Beings*, we having been Eye-Witnesses of this Matter almost every Day for a quarter of a Year together; so it may be a means to rectifie the depraved Judgment and Sentiments of other disbelieving Persons, and absolutely convince them of their Error, if they please to hear, without prejudice, the plain, but most true Narration of it; which was thus.

Some time ago being in *America*, (in His then Majesty's Service) I was lodg'd in the said *George Walton*'s House, a Planter there, and on a *Sunday* Night, about Ten a Clock, many Stones were heard by my self, and the rest of the Family, to be thrown, and (with Noise) hit against the top and all sides of the House, after he the said *Walton* had been at his Fence-Gate, which was between him and his Neighbour one *John Amazeen* an *Italian*, to view it; for it was again (as formerly it had been (the manner how being unknown) wrung off the Hinges, and cast upon the Ground; and in his being there, and return home with several Persons of (and frequenting) his family and House, about a flight shot distant from the Gate, they were all assaulted with a peal of Stones, (taken, we conceive, from the Rocks hard by the House) and this by unseen Hands or Agents. For by this time I was come down to them, having risen out of my Bed at this strange Alarm of all that were in the House, and do know that they all look'd out as narrowly as I did, or any Person could, (it being a bright Moon-light Night) but cou'd make no Discovery. Thereupon, and because there came many Stones, and those pretty great ones, some as big as my Fist, into the Entry or Porch of the House, we withdrew into the next Room to the Porch; no Person having receiv'd any Hurt, (praised be Almighty Providence, for certainly the infernal Agent, constant Enemy to Mankind, had he not been over-ruled, intended no less than Death or Maim) save only that two Youths were lightly hit, one on the Leg, the other on the Thigh, notwithstanding the Stones came so thick, and so forcibly against the sides of so narrow a Room. Whilst we stood amazed at this Accident, one of the Maidens imagined she saw them come from the Hall, next to that we were in, where searching, (and in the Cellar, down out of the Hall,) and finding no Body, another and my self observed two little Stones in a short space successively to fall on the Floor, coming

as.

as from the Ceiling clofe by us, and we concluded it muft ne-
ceffarily be done by means extraordinary and præternatural.
Coming again into the Room where we firft were, (next the
Porch) we had many of thefe lapidary Salutations, but unfriendly
ones; for, fhutting the Door, it was no fmall Surprife to me to
have a good big Stone come with great force and noife (juft by
my Head) againft the Door on the infide; and then fhutting
the other Door, next the Hall, to have the like Accident; fo
going out again, upon a neceffary Occafion, to have another
very near my Body, clattering againft the Board-wall of the
Houfe; but it was a much greater, to be fo near the danger of
having my Head broke with a Mall, or great Hammer brufhing
along the top or roof of the Room from the other end, as I was
walking in it, and lighting down by me; but it fell fo, that my
Landlord had the greateft damage, his Windows (efpecially
thofe of the firft mention'd Room) being with many Stones
miferably and ftrangely batter'd, moft of the Stones giving the
Blow on the infide, and forcing the Bars, Lead, and hafps of the
Cafements outwards, and yet falling back (fometimes a Yard
or two) into the Room; only one little Stone we took out of
the glafs of the Window, where it lodg'd its felf in the breaking
it, in a Hole exactly fit for the Stone. The Pewter and Brafs
were frequently pelted, and fometimes thrown down upon the
Ground; for the Evil Spirit feemed then to affect variety of
Mifchief, and diverted himfelf at this end after he had done fo
much Execution at the other. So were two Candlefticks, after
many hittings, at laft ftruck off the Table where they ftood,
and likewife a large Pewter Pot, with the force of thefe Stones.
Some of them were taken up hot, and (it feems) immediately
coming out of the Fire; and fome (which is not unremarkable)
having been laid by me upon the Table along by couples, and
numbred, were found miffing; that is, two of them, as we return'd immediately to the Table, having turn'd our backs only
to vifit and view fome new Stone-charge or Window-breach;
and this Experiment was four or five times repeated, and I ftill
found one or two miffing of the Number, which we all mark'd,
when I did but juft remove the Light from off the Table, and
ftep to the Door, and back again.

After this had continued in all the parts and fides of the firft
Room (and down the Chimney) for above four hours, I, weary
of the Noife, and fleepy, went to Bed, and was no fooner fallen
afleep,

afleep, but was awakened with the unwelcome difturbance of another Battery of a different fort, it iffuing with fo prodigious a Noife againft the thin Board-wall of my Chamber, (which was within another) that I could not imagin it lefs than the fracture and downfall of great part of the Chamber, or at leaft of the Shelves, Books, Pictures, and other things, placed on that fide, and on the Partition-Wall between the Anti-Chamber and the Door of mine. But the Noife immediately bringing up the Company below, they affured me no Mifchief of that nature was done, and fhewcd me the biggeft Stone that had as yet been made ufe of in this unaccountable Accident, weighing eight pound and an half, that had burft open my Chamber Door with a re-bound from the Floor, as by the Dent and Bruife in it near the Door I found next Morning, done, probably, to make the greater Noife, and give the more Aftonifhment, which would fooner be effected by three Motions, and confequently three feveral Sounds, *viz.* one on the Ground, the next to and on the Door, and the laft from it again to the Floor, then if it had been one fingle Blow upon the Door only; which ('tis probable) wou'd have fplit the Door, which was not permitted, nor fo much as a fquare of the Glafs-Window broken or crack'd (at that time) in all the Chamber. Glad thereof, and defiring them to leave me, and the Door fhut, as it was before, I endeavoured once more to take my Reft, and was once more prevented by the like paffage, with another like offenfive Weapon, it being a whole Brick that lay in the anti-Chamber Chimney, and ufed again to the fame ma-licious purpofe as before, and in the fame manner too, as by the mark in the Floor, whereon was fome of the duft of the Brick, broken a little at the end, apparant next Morning, the Brick it felf lying juft at the Door. However, after I had lain a while, harkning to their Adventures below, I drop'd afleep again, and receiv'd no further Moleftation that Night.

In the Morning (*Monday* Morning) I was inform'd by feveral of the Domefticks of more of the fame kind of Trouble; among which the moft fignal was, the Vanifhing of the Spit which ftood in the Chimney Corner, and the fudden coming of it again down the fame Chimney, fticking of it in a Log that lay in the Fire-place or Hearth; and then being by one of the Family fet by on the other fide of the Chimney, prefently caft out of the Window into the Back-fide. Alfo a preffing-Iron lying on the ledge of the Chimney back, was convey'd invifibly into the Yard. I

should

should think it (too) not unworthy the Relation, that, dif-
coursing then with some of the Family, and others, about what
had past, I said, I thought it necessary to take and keep the great
Stone, as a Proof and Evidence, for they had taken it down from
my Chambers; and so I carried it up, laid it on my Table in
my Chamber, and lock'd my Door, and going out upon occa-
sions, and soon returning, I was told by my Landlady that it
was, a little while after my going forth, removed again, with
a Noise, which they all below heard, and was thrown into the
anti-Chamber, and there I found it lying in the middle of it;
thereupon I the second time carried it up, and laid it on the
Table, and had it in my Custody a long time to show, for the
Satisfaction of the Curious.

There were many more Stones thrown about in the House that
Morning, and more in the Fields that Day, where the Master
of the House was, and the Men at Work. Some more Mr.
Woodbridge, a Minister, and my self, in the Afternoon did see,
(but could not any Hand throwing them) lighting near, and
jumping and tumbling on the Grass: So did one Mrs. *Clark*, and
her Son, and several others; and some of them felt them too.
One Person would not be perswaded but that the Boys at Work
might throw them, and strait her little Boy standing by her was
struck with a Stone on the Back, which caused him to fall a crying,
and her (being convinc'd) to carry him away forth-with.

In the Evening, as soon as I had sup'd in the outer Room before
mine, I took a little Musical-Instrument, and began to touch it,
(the Door indeed was then set open for Air) and a good big
Stone came rumbling in, and as it were to lead the Dance, but
upon a much different account than in the days of Old, and of
old fabulous Inchantments, my Musick being none of the best.
The Noise of this brought up the Deputy-President's Wife, and
many others of the Neighbourhood that were below, who wonder'd to see this Stone followed (as it were) by many others, and
a Pewter Spoon among the rest, all which fell strangely into the
Room in their Presence, and were taken up by the Company. And
beside all this, there was seen by two Youths in the Orchard and
Fields, as they said, a black Cat, at the time the Stones were toss'd
about, and it was shot at, but missed, by its changing Places, and
being immediately at some distance, and then out of sight, as they
related: Agreeable to which, it may not be improper to insert,
what was observed by two Maids, Grand-Children of Mr. *Walton* on
the

the *Sunday* Night, the beginning of this *Lithoboly*. They did affirm, that as they were ſtanding in the Porch-Chamber Window, they ſaw, as it were, a Perſon putting out a Hand out of the Hall Window, as throwing Stones toward the Porch or Entry; and we all know no Perſon was in the Hall except, at that inſtant, my ſelf and another, having ſearch'd diligently there, and wondring whence thoſe ſhould come that were about the ſame time drop'd near us; ſo far we were from doing it our ſelves, or ſeeing any other there to do it.

On *Monday* Night, about the Hour it firſt began there, were more Stones thrown in the Kitchin, and down the Chimney, one Captain *Bareſoot*, of the Council for that Province, being preſent, with others; and alſo (as I was going up to Bed) in an upper Chamber, and down thoſe Stairs.

Upon *Tueſday* Night, about Ten, ſome five or ſix Stones were ſeverally thrown into the Maid's Chamber near the Kitchin, and the Glaſs-Windows broke in three new places, and one of the Maids hit as ſhe lay. At the ſame time was heard by them, and two young Men in the Houſe, an odd, diſmal ſort of Whiſtling, and thereupon the Youths ran out, with intent to take the ſuppos'd Thrower of Stones, if poſſible; and on the back-ſide near the Window they heard the Noiſe (as they ſaid) of ſomething ſtepping a little way before them, as it were the trampling of a young Colt, as they fancied, but ſaw nothing; and going on, could diſcover nothing but that the Noiſe of the ſtepping or trampling was ceas'd, and then gone on a little before.

On *Saturday* Morning I found two Stones more on the Stairs; and ſo ſome were on *Sunday* Night convey'd into the Room next the Kitchin.

Upon *Monday* following Mr. *Walton* going (with his Men) by Water to ſome other Land, in a place called the *Great Bay*, and to a Houſe where his Son was placed, they lay there that Night, and the next Morning had this Adventure. As the Men were all at work in the Woods, felling Wood, they were viſited with another ſet of Stones, and they gathered up near upon a Hat-full, and put them between two Trees near adjoining, and returning from carrying Wood, to the Boat, the Hat and its contents (the Stones) were gone, and the Stones were preſently after thrown about again, as before; and after ſearch, found the Hat preſs'd together, and lying under a ſquare piece of Timber at ſome diſtance from thence. They had them again at young *Walton*'s
Houſe,

House, and half a Brick thrown into a Cradle, out of which his young Child was newly taken up.

Here it may seem most proper to inform the Reader of a parallel passage, (*viz.*) what happened another time to my Landlord in his Boat; wherein going up to the same place, (the *Great Bay*) and loading it with Hay for his use at his own House, about the mid-way in the River (*Pascataqua*) he found his Boat began to be in a sinking Condition, at which being much surpriz'd, upon search, he discover'd the cause to be the pulling out a Plug or Stopple in the bottom of the Boat, being fixed there for the more convenient letting out of the Rain-Water that might fall into it; a Contrivance and Combination of the old Serpent and the old Woman, or some other Witch or Wizard (in Revenge or innate Enmity) to have drown'd both my good Landlord and his Company.

On *Wednesday*, as they were at work again in the Woods, on a sudden they heard something gingle like Glass, or Metal, among the Trees, as it was falling, and being fallen to the Ground, they knew it to be a Stirrup which Mr. *Walton* had carried to the Boat, and laid under some Wood; and this being again laid by him in that very Boat, it was again thrown after him. The third time, he having put it upon his Girdle or Belt he wore about his Waste, buckled together before, but at that instant taken off because of the Heat of the Weather, and laid there again buckled, it was fetch'd away, and no more seen. Likewise the Graper, or little Anchor of the Boat, cast over-board, which caus'd the Boat to wind up; so staying and obstructing their Passage. Then the setting-Pole was divers times cast into the River, as they were coming back from the *Great Bay*, which put them to the trouble of Padling, *that is*, rowing about for it as often to retrieve it.

Being come to his own House, this Mr. *Walton* was charg'd again with a fresh Assault in the out-Houses; but we heard of none within doors until *Friday* after, when, in the Kitchin, were 4 or 5 Stones (one of them hot) taken out of the Fire, as I conceive, and so thrown about. I was then present, being newly come in with Mr. *Walton* from his middle Field, (as he call'd it) where his Servants had been Mowing, and had six or seven of his old troublesome Companions, and I had one fall'n down by me there, and another thin flat Stone hit me on the Thigh with the flat side of it, so as to make me just feel, and to smart a little. In the same Day's Evening, as I was walking out in the Lane by

the

the Field before-mentioned, a great Stone made a rufling Noife in the Stone-Fence between the Field and the Lane, which feem'd to me (as it caus'd me to caft my Eye that way by the Noife) to come out of the Fence, as it were pull'd out from among thofe Stones loofe, but orderly laid clofe together, as the manner of fuch Fences in that Country is, and fo fell down upon the Ground. Some Perfons of Note being then in the Field (whofe Names are here under-written) to vifit Mr. *Walton* there, are fubftantial Witneffes of this fame Stonery, both in the Field, and afterward in the Houfe that Night, *viz.* one Mr. *Huffey*, Son of a Coun-fellour there. He took up one that having firft alighted on the Ground, with rebound from thence hit him on the Heel; and he keeps it to fhow. And Captain *Barefoot*, mentioned above, has that which (among other Stones) flew into the Hall a little before Supper; which my felf alfo faw as it firft came in at the upper part of the Door into the middle of the Room; and then (tho' a good flat Stone, yet) was feen to rowl over and over, as if trundled, under a Bed in the fame Room. In fhort, thefe Perfons, being wonderoufly affected with the Strangenefs of thefe Paffages, offer'd themfelves (defiring me to take them) as Te-ftimonies; I did fo, and made a *Memorandum*, by way of Record, thereof, to this effect. *Viz.*

Thefe Perfons under-written do hereby Atteft the Truth of their being Eye-Witneffes of at leaft half a fcore Stone's that Evening thrown invifibly into the Field, and in the Entry of the Houfe, Hall, and one of the Chambers of George Walton's. *Viz.*

Samuel Jennings, *Efq; Governour of* Weft-Jarfey.
Walter Clark, *Efq; Deputy-Governour of* Road-Ifland.
Mr. Arthur Cook.
Mr. Matt. Borden *of* Road-Ifland.
Mr. Oliver Hooton *of* Barbados, *Merchant.*
Mr. T. Maul *of* Salem *in* New-England, *Merchant.*
Captain Walter Barefoot.
Mr. John Huffey.
And the Wife of the faid Mr. Huffey.

On *Saturday, July* 24. One of the Family, at the ufual hour at Night, obferv'd fome few (not above half a dozen) of thefe natural (or rather unnatural) Weapons to fly into the Kitchin, as formerly; but fome of them in an unufual manner lighting gently on him, or coming toward him fo eafily, as that he took them before they fell to the Ground. I think there was not any thing more that Night remarkable. But as if the malicious Dæmon had laid up for *Sunday* and *Monday*, then it was that he began (more furioufly than formerly) with a great Stone in the Kitchin, and fo continued with throwing down the Pewter-Difhes, &c. great part of it all at once coming clattering down, without the ftroke of a Stone, little or great, to move it. Then about Midnight this impious Operation not ceafing, but trefpaffing with *a continuando,* 2 very great Stones, weighing above 30 pound a piece, (that ufed to lye in the Kitchin, in or near the Chimny) were in the former, wonted, rebounding manner, let fly againft my Door and Wall in the ante-Chamber, but with fome little diftance of time. This thundring Noife muft needs bring up the Men from below, as before, (I need not fay to wake me) to tell me the Effect, which was the beating down feveral Pictures, and difplacing abundance of things about my Chamber: but the Repetition of this Cannon-Play by thefe great rumbling Engines, now ready at hand for the purpofe, and the like additional difturbance by four Bricks that lay in the outer-Room Chimney (one of which having been fo imploy'd the firft *Sunday* Night, as has been faid) made me defpair of taking Reft, and fo forced me to rife from my Bed. Then finding my Door burft open, I alfo found many Stones, and great pieces of Bricks, to fly in, breaking the Glafs-Windows, and a Paper-Light, fometimes inwards, fometimes outwards: So hitting the Door of my Chamber as I came through from the ante-Chamber, lighting very near me as I was fetching the Candleftick, and afterward the Candle being ftruck out, as I was going to light it again. So a little after, coming up for another Candle, and being at the Stare-foot door, a wooden Mortar with great Noife ftruck againft the Floor, and was juft at my Feet, only not touching me, moving from the other end of the Kitchin where it ufed to lye. And when I came up my felf, and two more of the fame Houfe, we heard a Whiftling, as it were near us in the outer Room, feveral times. Among the reft of the Tools made ufe of to difturb us, I found an old Card for dreffing Flax in my Chamber. Now for *Monday* Night, (*June* 26)

one

one of the feverest. The difturbance began in the Kitchin with Stones; then as I was at Supper above in the ante-Chamber, the Window near which I fate at Table was broke in 2 or 3 parts of it inwards, and one of the Stones that broke it flew in, and I took it up at the further end of the Room. The manner is obfervable; for one of the fquares was broke into 9 or 10 fmall fquare pieces, as if it had been regularly mark'd out into fuch even fquares by a Workman, to the end fome of thefe little pieces might fly in my Face, (as they did) and give me a furprize, but without any hurt. In the mean time it went on in the Kitchin, whither I went down, for Company, all or moft of the Family, and a Neighbour, being there; where many Stones (fome great ones) came thick and threefold among us, and an old howing Iron, from a Room hard by, where fuch Utenfils lay. Then, as if I had been the defign'd Object for that time, moft of the Stones that came (the fmaller I mean) hit me, (fometimes pretty hard) to the number of above 20, near 30, as I remember, and whether I remov'd, fit, or walk'd, I had them, and great ones fometimes lighting gently on me, and in my Hand and Lap as I fate, and falling to the Ground, and fometimes thumping againft the Wall, as near as could be to me, without touching me. Then was a Room over the Kitchin infefted, that had not been fo before, and many Stones greater than ufual lumbring there over our Heads, not only to ours, but to the great Difturbance and Affrightment of fome Children that lay there. And for Variety, there were fometimes three great, diftinct Knocks, fometimes five fuch founds as with a great Maul, reiterated divers times.

On *Tuefday* Night (*June* 28) we were quiet; but not fo on *Wednefday*, when the Stones were play'd about in the Houfe. And on *Thurfday* Morning I found fome things that hung on Nails on the Wall in my Chamber, viz. a Spherical Sun-Dial, &c. lying on the Ground, as knock'd down by fome Brick or Stone in the ante-Chamber. But my Landlord had the worft of that Day, tho' he kept the Field, being there invifibly hit above 40 times, as he affirm'd to me, and he receiv'd fome fhrowd hurtful-Blows on the Back, and other Parts, which he much complained of, and faid he thought he fhould have reafon to do, even to his dying day; and I obferv'd that he did fo, he being departed this Life fince.

Befides this, Plants of *Indian* Corn were ftruck up by the Roots almoft, juft as if they had been cut with fome edged Inftrument, whereas *re vera* they were feen to be eradicated, or rooted up with nothing

nothing but the very Stones, altho' the injurious Agent was altogether unseen. And a sort of Noise, like that of Snorting and Whistling, was heard near the Men at Work in the Fields many times, many whereof I my self, going thither, and being there, was a Witness of; and parting thence I receiv'd a pretty hard Blow with a Stone on the Calf of my Leg. So it continued that day in two Fields, where they were severally at Work: and my Landlord told me, he often heard likewise a humming Noise in the Air by him, as of a Bullet discharg'd from a Gun; and so said a Servant of his that work'd with him.

Upon *Saturday*, (*July* 1) as I was going to visit my Neighbour Capt. *Barefoot*, and just at his Door his Man saw, as well as my self, 3 or 4 Stones fall just by us in the Field, or Close, where the House stands, and not any other Person near us. At Night a great Stone fell in the Kitchin, as I was going to Bed, and the Pewter was thrown down; many Stones flew about, and the Candles by them put out 3 or 4 times, and the Snorting heard; a Negro Maid hit on the Head in the Entry between the Kitchin and Hall with a Porringer from the Kitchin: also the pressing-Iron clatter'd against the Partition Wall between the Hall and a Chamber beyond it, where I lay, and Mr. *Randolph*, His Majesty's Officer for the Customs, *&c.*

Some few Stones we had on *Sunday* Morning, (*July* 2) none at Night. But on *Monday* Morning (the 3*d*) both Mr. *Walton*, and 5 or 6 with him in the Field, were assaulted with them, and their Ears with the old Snorting and Whistling. In the Afternoon Mr. *Walton* was hit on the Back with Stones very grievously, as he was in his Boat that lay at a Cove side by his House. It was a very odd prank that was practis'd by the Devil a little while after this. One Night the Cocks of Hay, made the Day before in the Orchard, was spread all abroad, and some of the Hay thrown up into the Trees, and some of it brought into the House, and scatter'd. Two Logs that lay at the Door, laid, one of them by the Chimny in the Kitchin; the other set against the Door of the Room where Mr. *Walton* then lay, as on purpose to confine him therein: A Form that stood in the Entry (or Porch) was set along by the Fire side, and a joint Stool upon that, with a Napkin spread thereon, with two Pewter Pots, and two Candlesticks: A Cheese-Press likewise having a Spit thrust into one of the holes of it, at one end; and at the other end of the Spit hung an Iron Kettle; and a Cheese was taken out, and broke to pieces.

Another

Another time, I full well remember 'twas on a *Sunday* at Night, my Window was all broke with a violent shock of Stones and Brick-bats, which scarce miss'd my self: among these one huge one made its way through the great square or shash of a Casement, and broke a great hole in it, throwing down Books by the way, from the Window to a Picture over-against it, on the other side of the Chamber, and tore a hole quite through it about half a foot long, and the piece of the Cloth hung by a little part of it, on the back-side of the Picture.

After this we were pretty quiet, saving now and then a few Stones march'd about for Exercise, and to keep (as it were) the Diabolical hand in use, till *July* 28, being *Friday*, when about 40 Stones flew about, abroad, and in the House and Orchard, and among the Trees therein, and a Window broke before, was broke again, and one Room where they never used before.

August 1. On *Wednesday* the Window in my ante-Chamber was broke again, and many Stones were plaid about, abroad, and in the House, in the Day-time, and at Night. The same Day in the Morning they tried this Experiment; they did set on the Fire a Pot with Urin, and crooked Pins in it, with design to have it boil, and by that means to give Punishment to the Witch, or Wizard, (that might be the wicked Procurer or Contriver of this Stone Affliction) and take off their own; as they had been advised. This was the Effect of it: As the Liquor begun to grow hot, a Stone came and broke the top or mouth of it, and threw it down, and spilt what was in it; which being made good again, another Stone, as the Pot grew hot again, broke the handle off; and being recruited and fill'd the third time, was then with a third Stone quite broke to pieces and split; and so the Operation became frustrate and fruitless.

On *August* 2. two Stones in the Afternoon I heard and saw my self in the House and Orchard; and another Window in the Hall was broke. And as I was entring my own Chamber, a great square of a Casement, being a foot square, was broke, with the Noise as of a big Stone, and pieces of the Glass flew into the Room, but no Stone came in then, or could be found within or without. At Night, as I, with others, were in the Kitchin, many more came in; and one great Stone that lay on a Spinning-Wheel to keep it steady, was thrown to the other side of the Room. Several Neighbours then present were ready to testifie this Matter.

Upon

Upon *August* 3. On *Thursday* the Gate between my said Landlord and his Neighbour *John Amazeen* was taken off again, and thrown into *Amazeen*'s Field, who heard it fall, and averr'd it then made a Noise like a great Gun.

On *Friday* the 4th, the Fence against Mr. *Walton*'s Neighbour's Door, (the Woman of whom formerly there was great Suspicion, and thereupon Examination had, as appears upon Record ;) this Fence being maliciously pull'd down to let in their Cattel into his Ground ; he and his Servants were pelted with above 40 Stones as they went to put it up again ; for she had often threatned that he should never injoy his House and Land. Mr. *Walton* was hit divers times, and all that Day in the Field, as they were Reaping, it ceas'd not, and their fell (by the Mens Computation) above an hundred Stones. A Woman helping to Reap (among the rest) was hit 9 or 10 times, and hurt to that degree, that her left Arm, Hip, Thigh, and Leg, were made black and blue therewith ; which she showd to the Woman, Mrs. *Walton*, and others. Mr. *Woodbridge*, a Divine, coming to give me a Visit, was hit about the Hip, and one Mr. *Jefferys* a Merchant, who was with him, on the Leg. A Window in the Kitchin that had been much batter'd before, was now quite broke out, and unwindow'd, no Glass or Lead at all being left : a Glass Bottle broke to pieces, and the Pewter Dishes (about 9 of them) thrown down, and bent.

On *Saturday* the 5th, as they were Reaping in the Field, three Sickles were crack'd and broke by the force of these lapidary Instruments of the Devil, as the Sickles were in the Reapers hands, on purpose (it seems) to obstruct their Labour, and do them Injury and Damage. And very many Stones were cast about that Day ; insomuch, that some that assisted at that Harvest-Work, being struck with them, by reason of that Disturbance left the Field, but were follow'd by their invisible Adversaries to the next House.

On *Sunday*, being the 6th, there fell nothing considerable, nor on *Monday*, (7th) save only one of the Children hit with a Stone on the Back. We were quiet to *Tuesday* the 8th. But on *Wednesday* (9th) above 100 Stones (as they verily thought) repeated the Reapers Disquiet in the Corn-Field, whereof some were affirm'd by Mr. *Walton* to be great ones indeed, near as big as a Man's Head ; and Mrs. *Walton*, his Wife, being by Curiosity led thither, with intent also to make some Discovery by the most diligent and vigilant Observation she could use, to obviate the

idle

idle Incredulity fome inconfiderate Perfons might irrationally entertain concerning this venefical Operation; or at leaft to confirm her own Sentiments and Belief of it. Which fhe did, but to her Coft; for fhe received an untoward Blow (with a Stone) on her Shoulder. There were likewife two Sickles bent, crack'd, and difabled with them, beating them violently out of their Hands that held them; and this reiterated three times fucceffively.

After this we injoy'd our former Peace and Quiet, unmolefted by thefe ftony Difturbances, that whole Month of *Auguft*, excepting fome few times; and the laft of all in the Month of *September*, (the beginning thereof) wherein Mr. *Walton* himfelf only (the Original perhaps of this ftrange Adventure, as has been declared) was the defigned concluding Sufferer; who going in his Canoo (or Boat) from the *Great Ifland*, where he dwelt, to *Portfmouth*, to attend the Council; who had taken Cognizance of this Matter, he being Summoned thither, in order to his and the Sufpect's Examination, and the Courts taking Order thereabout, he was fadly hit with three pebble Stones as big as ones Fift; one of which broke his Head, which I faw him fhow to the Prefident of the Council; the others gave him that Pain on the Back, of which (with other like Strokes) he complained then; and afterward to his Death.

Who, that perufes thefe præternatural Occurrences, can poffibly be fo much an Enemy to his own Soul, and irrefutable Reafon, as obftinately to oppofe himfelf to, or confufedly fluctuate in, the Opinion and Doctrine of *Dæmons*, or *Spirits*, and *Witches*? Certainly he that do's fo, muft do two things more: He muft temerarioufly unhinge, or undermine the Fundamentals of the beft Religion in the World; and he muft difingenuoufly quit and abandon that of the Three Theologick Virtues or Graces, to which the great Doctor of the *Gentils* gave the Precedence, *Charity*, through his Unchriftian and Uncharitable Incredulity.

FINIS.